MASTER
EXCEL

Your Ultimate Guide to Mastering Functions,
Formulas, and More!

VIRAJ KAKADIA

Master Excel 2025: Your Ultimate Guide to Mastering Functions, Formulas, and More!

Table of Contents

Master Excel 2025: Your Ultimate Guide to Mastering Functions, Formulas, and More!

Master Excel 2025: Your Ultimate Guide to Mastering Functions, Formulas, and More!

Master Excel 2025: Your Ultimate Guide to Mastering Functions, Formulas, and More!

Disclaimer

Copyright © 2024 by Viraj Kakadia

ISBN: 9798324235901

Introduction

Welcome to "Master Excel 2025: Your Ultimate Guide to Mastering Functions, Formulas, and More! Step-by-Step Tutorials, Real-world Examples, and Expert Tips & Tricks Included." In this comprehensive eBook, you will embark on a journey to unlock the full potential of Excel, the world's leading spreadsheet software. Whether you're a beginner looking to grasp the basics or an experienced user seeking advanced techniques, this guide has something for everyone.

Throughout this eBook, you will find step-by-step tutorials, real-world examples, and expert tips and tricks to help you become proficient in Excel 2025. From mastering essential functions and formulas to leveraging advanced features for data analysis and visualization, you'll gain the skills needed to excel in various personal, academic, and professional endeavors.

So, let's dive in and unleash the power of Excel together!

Chapter 1: Getting Started with Excel

Excel is a powerful tool that allows you to organize, analyze, and visualize data with ease. Whether you're managing finances, tracking inventory, or creating reports, Excel provides a wide range of features to help you accomplish your tasks efficiently.

What is Excel?

Excel is a spreadsheet program developed by Microsoft that allows users to enter, manipulate, and analyze data using a grid of cells arranged in rows and columns. It offers a variety of functions and formulas for performing calculations, as well as tools for creating charts and graphs to visualize data.

Understanding the Excel Interface

When you open Excel, you'll be greeted by the familiar interface consisting of the Ribbon, Quick Access Toolbar, and the workbook area. The Ribbon contains tabs, each of which displays a set of commands related to specific tasks, such as formatting, inserting, and analyzing data.

The workbook area is where you'll work with your data. It consists of individual worksheets, each represented by a tab at the bottom of the window. You can navigate between worksheets by clicking on their respective tabs.

Navigating Worksheets and Workbooks

Navigating worksheets and workbooks in Excel is straightforward. To move between worksheets within a workbook, simply click on the tabs at the bottom of the window. You can also use the keyboard shortcuts Ctrl + Page Up and Ctrl + Page Down to navigate between worksheets.

To navigate between different workbooks, you can use the Switch Windows button located on the View tab of the Ribbon. This allows you to easily switch between open workbooks without closing any of them.

Entering Data

Entering data into Excel is simple. You can click on any cell and start typing to enter text or numbers. Pressing Enter will move you to the cell below, while pressing Tab will move you to the cell to the right.

Formatting Cells

Excel offers a wide range of formatting options to make your data more visually appealing and easier to understand. You can format cells to change the font style, size, color, alignment, and more. Additionally, you can apply number formats to display values as currency, percentages, dates, and more.

Working with Rows and Columns

You can insert, delete, and resize rows and columns in Excel to adjust the layout of your data. To insert a row or column, right-click on the row or column header where you want to insert it and select the appropriate option from the context menu. To delete a row or column, select it and press the Delete key on your keyboard.

Saving and Closing Workbooks

It's important to save your work regularly to avoid losing any changes. To save a workbook, click on the File tab in the Ribbon and select Save or Save As. Choose a location on your computer to save the file, enter a name for the file, and click Save.

To close a workbook, click on the File tab and select Close. If you have made any changes to the workbook since the last time you saved it, Excel will prompt you to save your changes before closing the workbook.

Chapter 2: Essential Functions and Formulas

In Excel, functions and formulas are the building blocks for performing calculations and manipulating data. Understanding how to use them effectively is essential for mastering Excel.

Introduction to Functions

A function in Excel is a predefined formula that performs a specific task. Functions take arguments, or input values, and return a result. Excel offers a wide range of built-in functions for performing various mathematical, statistical, logical, and text manipulation tasks.

Basic Formulas for Calculations

Formulas in Excel always start with an equal sign (=) followed by the formula expression. You can use basic arithmetic operators such as addition (+), subtraction (-), multiplication (*), and division (/) to perform calculations. For example, to add two numbers, you would enter a formula like =A1+B1, where A1 and B1 are the cell references containing the numbers you want to add.

Using Built-in Functions

Excel provides a vast library of built-in functions that can save you time and effort when performing complex calculations. Some common functions include SUM,

AVERAGE, MAX, MIN, COUNT, and IF. To use a function, simply type its name followed by the arguments enclosed in parentheses. For example, the SUM function calculates the sum of a range of cells: =SUM(A1:A10).

Excel functions can be nested within each other to perform more advanced calculations. For example, you can use the IF function to perform a logical test and return different values based on whether the test is true or false. Nested functions allow you to create complex formulas that automate tasks and streamline your workflow.

Practical Examples

Let's explore some practical examples to illustrate the use of functions and formulas in Excel:

1. Calculating Total Sales: Suppose you have a dataset containing sales figures for different products. You can use the SUM function to calculate the total sales for all products.

2. Finding the Average: If you have a list of test scores, you can use the AVERAGE function to find the average score.

3. Conditional Formatting: You can use conditional formatting to highlight cells that meet specific criteria. For example, you can apply formatting to cells that contain values above a certain threshold.

Master Excel 2025: Your Ultimate Guide to Mastering Functions, Formulas, and More!

Expert Tips & Tricks

- Use named ranges to make your formulas more readable and easier to understand.

- Learn keyboard shortcuts for commonly used functions to improve your efficiency.

- Explore Excel's Function Library to discover new functions and capabilities.

By mastering essential functions and formulas, you'll be able to tackle a wide range of tasks in Excel and unlock its full potential for data analysis and manipulation.

Chapter 3: Advanced Functions and Formulas

In this chapter, we'll delve deeper into Excel's advanced functions and formulas, empowering you to tackle complex calculations and data manipulation tasks with confidence.

Advanced Mathematical Functions

Excel offers a plethora of advanced mathematical functions that cater to diverse analytical needs. These functions include trigonometric functions like SIN, COS, and TAN, exponential and logarithmic functions like EXP and LOG, as well as statistical functions like STDEV, VAR, and CORREL. Understanding how to leverage these functions can greatly enhance your analytical capabilities.

Logical Functions for Decision Making

Logical functions in Excel allow you to make decisions based on specified conditions. The IF function, for instance, evaluates a condition and returns one value if the condition is true and another value if it is false. Other logical functions such as AND, OR, and NOT enable more complex decision-making scenarios, empowering you to automate processes and streamline workflows.

Text Functions for Manipulating Text

Text functions in Excel enable you to manipulate and extract information from text strings. Whether you need to concatenate strings, extract substrings, convert text to uppercase or lowercase, or find specific characters within a string, Excel's text functions have you covered. Mastering these functions will allow you to efficiently manage textual data within your spreadsheets.

Practical Examples

To illustrate the utility of advanced functions and formulas, let's consider a few practical examples:

1. Forecasting Sales: Utilize Excel's statistical functions such as TREND or FORECAST to predict future sales based on historical data.

2. Conditional Aggregation: Combine logical functions like IF and SUMIFS to perform conditional aggregation, such as calculating the total sales for a specific product category within a certain date range.

3. Text Parsing: Employ text functions like LEFT, RIGHT, and MID to parse and extract relevant information from textual data, such as extracting the first name from a full name string.

Expert Tips & Tricks

- Use the Insert Function dialog box (fx) to explore and insert functions into your formulas accurately.

Master Excel 2025: Your Ultimate Guide to Mastering Functions, Formulas, and More!

- Utilize array formulas to perform calculations across multiple cells or ranges efficiently.

- Experiment with Excel's Function Wizard to understand the syntax and functionality of various functions.

By harnessing the power of advanced functions and formulas, you'll be equipped to tackle even the most intricate analytical challenges in Excel.

Chapter 4: Data Analysis with Excel

Excel is not just a tool for organizing data; it's also a powerful platform for analyzing and deriving insights from your datasets. In this chapter, we'll explore various techniques for data analysis using Excel's built-in features.

Sorting and Filtering Data

Sorting and filtering are fundamental data analysis techniques that allow you to organize and focus on specific subsets of your data. Excel provides robust sorting and filtering capabilities, enabling you to arrange your data in ascending or descending order based on one or more criteria, as well as filter out rows that meet certain conditions.

Creating PivotTables for Summarizing Data

PivotTables are one of Excel's most powerful features for data summarization and analysis. With PivotTables, you can quickly summarize large datasets, identify trends, and generate insightful reports without the need for complex formulas. PivotTables allow you to pivot, or rotate, data from rows to columns or vice versa, facilitating dynamic analysis and exploration.

Performing What-If Analysis with Scenarios

What-If Analysis allows you to explore different scenarios and understand how changes in input variables affect the outcomes of your calculations. Excel offers several tools for performing What-If Analysis, including Scenario Manager, Goal Seek, and Data Tables. These tools empower you to make informed decisions and optimize your strategies based on hypothetical situations.

Practical Examples

Let's consider some practical examples of data analysis in Excel:

1. Sales Performance Analysis: Use sorting and filtering to identify top-performing products or sales representatives, and leverage PivotTables to analyze sales trends across different regions or time periods.

2. Budget Planning: Perform What-If Analysis to assess the impact of varying expense levels or revenue projections on your budget, allowing you to make informed decisions and adjustments accordingly.

3. Inventory Management: Utilize PivotTables to summarize inventory data, identify slow-moving or overstocked items, and optimize inventory levels to minimize holding costs.

Expert Tips & Tricks

- Use Excel Tables (Ctrl + T) to convert your data into structured tables, making it easier to sort, filter, and analyze.

- Take advantage of PivotTable slicers to interactively filter and analyze data, enhancing usability and visual appeal.

- Experiment with different scenarios using Scenario Manager to understand the potential outcomes of various decisions or events.

By mastering data analysis techniques in Excel, you'll be able to uncover valuable insights, make informed decisions, and drive business success.

Chapter 5: Visualizing Data with Charts

In this chapter, we'll explore the power of data visualization using Excel's charting capabilities. Charts are an effective way to communicate insights and trends in your data, making complex information more accessible and understandable.

Creating Basic Charts

Excel offers a variety of chart types to suit different data visualization needs, including column charts, bar charts, line charts, pie charts, and more. Creating a basic chart in Excel is straightforward: select your data, choose the desired chart type from the Insert tab in the Ribbon, and customize the chart elements as needed.

Customizing Chart Elements

Excel provides extensive options for customizing chart elements to enhance their clarity and visual appeal. You can modify chart titles, axis labels, data series, colors, and styles to effectively convey your message. Additionally, you can add data labels, trendlines, and annotations to provide context and insight into your charts.

Using Sparklines for Data Visualization

Sparklines are small, compact charts that can be embedded directly within cells, allowing you to visualize trends and patterns alongside your data.

Excel offers three types of Sparklines: Line Sparklines, Column Sparklines, and Win/Loss Sparklines. These miniature charts provide a quick and intuitive way to spot trends and variations in your data.

Practical Examples

Let's explore some practical examples of data visualization using Excel charts:

1. Sales Trend Analysis: Create a line chart to visualize sales trends over time, enabling you to identify seasonal patterns, fluctuations, and growth trends.

2. Market Share Comparison: Use a pie chart or a stacked column chart to compare the market share of different products or competitors, helping you understand your company's position in the market.

3. Budget vs. Actual Analysis: Generate a combination chart to compare budgeted and actual expenses or revenues across different categories, facilitating variance analysis and decision-making.

Expert Tips & Tricks

- Choose the most appropriate chart type based on the nature of your data and the insights you want to convey.

- Use chart templates to save time and maintain consistency in your visualizations.

- Experiment with different chart layouts, styles, and colors to find the most effective representation for your data.

By mastering data visualization techniques in Excel, you'll be able to communicate your findings effectively, drive understanding and decision-making, and unlock the full potential of your data.

Chapter 6: Enhancing Productivity with Excel

Excel offers a plethora of features and functionalities designed to enhance productivity and streamline workflows. In this chapter, we'll explore various techniques and tools that can help you work more efficiently and effectively with your data.

Data Validation Techniques

Data validation allows you to control the type and format of data entered into your spreadsheets, reducing errors and ensuring data integrity. Excel offers several data validation techniques, including dropdown lists, date restrictions, and custom validation rules. By implementing data validation, you can improve the accuracy and reliability of your data.

Using Macros for Automation

Macros are powerful automation tools that allow you to record and replay sequences of actions in Excel. With macros, you can automate repetitive tasks, such as formatting, data entry, and report generation, saving time and reducing the risk of errors. Excel's built-in Visual Basic for Applications (VBA) editor enables you to write custom macros to suit your specific needs.

Collaborating with Others in Excel

Excel provides features for collaborative work, allowing multiple users to work on the same workbook simultaneously. You can share workbooks via OneDrive or SharePoint, track changes made by different users, and merge conflicting changes using Excel's collaboration tools. Additionally, you can protect sensitive information and restrict access to certain parts of your workbook to maintain data security.

Practical Examples

Let's explore some practical examples of enhancing productivity with Excel:

1. Automating Reporting Tasks: Record a macro to automate the generation of weekly or monthly reports, including data import, formatting, and chart creation.

2. Streamlining Data Entry: Use data validation to create dropdown lists for selecting options, ensuring consistent data entry and minimizing errors.

3. Collaborative Budgeting: Share a budget workbook with team members, allowing them to input their budget estimates and track changes in real-time, facilitating collaborative budget planning.

Expert Tips & Tricks

- Use keyboard shortcuts to perform common tasks quickly and efficiently.

Master Excel 2025: Your Ultimate Guide to Mastering Functions, Formulas, and More!

- Explore Excel's Add-ins and third-party tools to extend its functionality and streamline your workflow.

- Regularly update and maintain your macros to ensure compatibility and reliability with new Excel versions.

By leveraging Excel's productivity features, you can optimize your workflows, increase efficiency, and accomplish more in less time.

Chapter 7: Tips and Tricks for Excel Mastery

In this chapter, we'll uncover a treasure trove of tips and tricks to help you master Excel and become a more efficient and proficient user. These tips range from keyboard shortcuts to advanced techniques that can save you time and enhance your productivity.

Keyboard Shortcuts for Efficiency

Keyboard shortcuts are a fast and efficient way to navigate Excel and perform common tasks without lifting your hands off the keyboard. Whether you're formatting cells, navigating worksheets, or performing calculations, learning keyboard shortcuts can significantly speed up your workflow. Excel offers a wide range of keyboard shortcuts for various commands and functions, allowing you to work more efficiently.

Time-Saving Techniques

Excel offers several time-saving techniques that can help you streamline your workflow and accomplish tasks more quickly. These techniques include using Autofill to fill in series of data, using the Flash Fill feature to automatically extract and format data, and using Quick Analysis to quickly visualize and analyze your data. By mastering these techniques, you can save time and focus on more important aspects of your work.

Troubleshooting Common Issues

Despite its robustness, Excel may encounter issues or errors that can hinder your productivity. Knowing how to troubleshoot common issues can help you resolve problems quickly and get back on track. Whether it's dealing with formula errors, handling large datasets, or optimizing performance, understanding common issues and their solutions is essential for Excel mastery.

Practical Examples

Let's explore some practical examples of tips and tricks for Excel mastery:

1. Using Ctrl + Arrow Keys to navigate quickly to the edge of data ranges.

2. Pressing Ctrl + Shift + L to toggle the Autofilter feature for filtering data.

3. Pressing F2 to edit a cell directly without double-clicking.

Expert Tips & Tricks

- Customize Excel's settings and options to suit your preferences and workflow.

- Explore Excel's online resources, including forums, tutorials, and help documentation, for additional tips and insights.

Master Excel 2025: Your Ultimate Guide to Mastering Functions, Formulas, and More!

- Practice regularly and experiment with new features and techniques to continually improve your Excel skills.

By incorporating these tips and tricks into your Excel workflow, you'll become a more proficient user and unlock the full potential of this powerful spreadsheet software.

Chapter 8: Mastering Excel for Specialized Tasks

In this chapter, we'll explore how to leverage Excel for specialized tasks across various domains, including finance, statistics, and project management. By mastering Excel for specialized tasks, you'll be equipped to tackle specific challenges and excel in your professional endeavors.

Financial Analysis with Excel

Excel is widely used in finance for tasks such as budgeting, forecasting, and financial modeling. In this section, we'll explore techniques for performing financial analysis in Excel, including calculating key financial metrics, creating cash flow forecasts, and conducting scenario analysis. Whether you're a financial analyst, accountant, or business owner, mastering financial analysis in Excel is essential for informed decision-making and strategic planning.

Statistical Analysis Techniques

Excel provides a range of statistical functions and tools for analyzing data and deriving insights. In this section, we'll delve into statistical analysis techniques such as descriptive statistics, hypothesis testing, regression analysis, and ANOVA (analysis of variance). Understanding how to apply statistical analysis techniques in Excel can help you make data-driven decisions, identify trends and patterns, and uncover relationships within your data.

Project Management Tools in Excel

Excel can also serve as a powerful tool for project management, allowing you to plan, track, and manage projects effectively. In this section, we'll explore project management techniques using Excel, including creating Gantt charts, tracking tasks and milestones, and analyzing project progress. Whether you're a project manager, team leader, or freelancer, mastering project management in Excel can help you stay organized, meet deadlines, and deliver successful outcomes.

Practical Examples

Let's consider some practical examples of using Excel for specialized tasks:

1. Financial Modeling: Build a dynamic financial model in Excel to analyze investment opportunities, forecast financial performance, and assess business valuations.

2. Statistical Analysis: Conduct a hypothesis test in Excel to determine whether there is a significant difference between two sample means, helping you make informed decisions based on statistical evidence.

3. Project Planning: Create a Gantt chart in Excel to visualize project timelines, identify critical

path activities, and allocate resources effectively, ensuring timely project completion.

Expert Tips & Tricks

- Use Excel's What-If Analysis tools, such as Goal Seek and Scenario Manager, to analyze the impact of different variables on project outcomes and financial performance.

- Utilize Excel's built-in templates and add-ins for specialized tasks, such as financial modeling templates or project management add-ins.

- Learn advanced Excel techniques, such as array formulas and data tables, to perform complex calculations and analyses efficiently.

By mastering Excel for specialized tasks, you'll be equipped to tackle diverse challenges and excel in your professional role, whether in finance, statistics, project management, or beyond.

Chapter 9: Excel in the Real World

In this chapter, we'll explore how Excel is utilized in real-world scenarios across various domains, including business, academia, and personal finance. Understanding Excel's practical applications in the real world can help you maximize its utility and relevance in your professional and personal life.

Excel in Business Environments

Excel is widely used in business environments for tasks such as data analysis, reporting, and decision support. In this section, we'll explore how businesses leverage Excel to manage finances, track sales and inventory, analyze market trends, and generate reports. Whether you work in finance, marketing, operations, or any other business function, Excel is likely to be an indispensable tool in your toolkit.

Excel in Academia

Excel is also extensively used in academia for tasks such as data analysis, research, and teaching. In this section, we'll explore how educators and researchers utilize Excel to analyze experimental data, create interactive learning materials, and conduct simulations. Whether you're a student, researcher, or educator, Excel can be a valuable tool for enhancing learning, conducting research, and presenting findings.

Excel in Personal Finance Management

Excel is not just for professional use; it's also a powerful tool for personal finance management. In this section, we'll explore how individuals use Excel to create budgets, track expenses, manage investments, and plan for financial goals. Whether you're managing household finances, planning for retirement, or tracking investments, Excel can help you take control of your financial future.

Practical Examples

Let's consider some practical examples of Excel's real-world applications:

1. Business Analysis: Analyze sales data to identify top-performing products, forecast future sales trends, and optimize marketing strategies.

2. Academic Research: Analyze experimental data to test hypotheses, visualize research findings, and generate publication-quality graphs and charts.

3. Personal Finance Management: Create a budget spreadsheet to track income and expenses, monitor savings goals, and plan for major expenses such as vacations or home renovations.

Expert Tips & Tricks

- Customize Excel's features and settings to suit your specific needs and preferences.

**<u>Master Excel 2025: Your Ultimate Guide to Mastering
Functions, Formulas, and More!</u>**

- Take advantage of Excel's collaboration features to work with colleagues or family members on shared projects or budgets.

- Explore Excel's online community forums and resources for tips, tutorials, and solutions to common challenges.

By understanding Excel's practical applications in the real world, you can harness its full potential to drive success in your professional endeavors and personal life.

Chapter 10: Excel in the Future

In this final chapter, we'll explore the future of Excel and how it is evolving to meet the needs of users in an increasingly digital and interconnected world. From emerging trends to integration with other technologies, Excel continues to evolve and adapt to remain a vital tool for data analysis, visualization, and decision-making.

Emerging Trends in Excel Usage

Excel usage is evolving rapidly, driven by advancements in technology and changes in user preferences. In this section, we'll explore emerging trends in Excel usage, such as the adoption of cloud-based solutions, the rise of mobile apps, and the integration of artificial intelligence and machine learning capabilities. Understanding these trends can help you stay ahead of the curve and leverage Excel's latest features and functionalities.

Excel Integration with Other Tools

Excel's versatility extends beyond its standalone capabilities, as it integrates seamlessly with a wide range of other tools and technologies. In this section, we'll explore how Excel integrates with other Microsoft Office applications, such as Word and PowerPoint, as well as third-party software and platforms. Whether you're importing data from external sources, collaborating with colleagues, or presenting insights to stakeholders, Excel's integration capabilities enhance its utility and effectiveness.

Excel's Role in the Digital Age

In an era characterized by data-driven decision-making and digital transformation, Excel remains a cornerstone tool for businesses, educators, researchers, and individuals alike. In this section, we'll reflect on Excel's enduring relevance and its role in empowering users to analyze data, derive insights, and make informed decisions. Despite the emergence of new technologies and tools, Excel continues to play a central role in facilitating productivity, collaboration, and innovation.

Conclusion

As we conclude our journey through "Master Excel 2025: Your Ultimate Guide to Mastering Functions, Formulas, and More!", we're reminded of Excel's enduring legacy as a versatile and indispensable tool for data analysis, visualization, and decision-making. Whether you're a beginner exploring Excel's basic functionalities or an advanced user leveraging its advanced features, Excel offers limitless possibilities for unlocking insights and driving success in your personal and professional endeavors. As Excel continues to evolve and adapt to meet the changing needs of users, we look forward to embracing its future innovations and capabilities.

Appendix: Additional Resources

In this appendix, you'll find a curated list of additional resources to further enhance your Excel skills and knowledge. Whether you're looking for tutorials, reference guides, or online communities, these resources can serve as valuable supplements to your learning journey.

Online Tutorials and Courses

- Microsoft Excel Official Training: Access free tutorials and courses directly from Microsoft to learn Excel fundamentals and advanced techniques.

- LinkedIn Learning: Explore a wide range of Excel courses on LinkedIn Learning, covering topics such as data analysis, formulas, and macros.

- Udemy: Browse Udemy's extensive collection of Excel courses taught by industry experts, with options for all skill levels and learning styles.

Books and Reference Guides

- "Excel 2025 for Dummies" by Greg Harvey: A comprehensive guide to mastering Excel's features and functionalities, suitable for beginners and experienced users alike.

- "Excel Formulas and Functions: Step-by-Step Guide with Examples" by Adam Ramirez: An in-depth exploration of Excel formulas and functions, accompanied by practical examples and explanations.

- "Power Excel with MrExcel: Master Pivot Tables, Subtotals, Charts, VLOOKUP, IF, Data Analysis in Excel 2010–2025" by Bill Jelen: Unlock the full potential of Excel with tips and techniques from Excel expert Bill Jelen, also known as MrExcel.

Online Communities and Forums

- Stack Overflow: Join the Excel community on Stack Overflow to ask questions, share knowledge, and collaborate with other users.

- Reddit r/excel: Engage with fellow Excel enthusiasts on Reddit's r/excel community, where you can find tips, tricks, and solutions to common Excel challenges.

- Exceljet: Explore Excel tutorials, tips, and keyboard shortcuts on Exceljet, a comprehensive resource for Excel users of all levels.

Excel Add-ins and Tools

- Power Query: Explore, transform, and analyze data from various sources with Power Query, a powerful data connectivity tool available in Excel.

- Power Pivot: Analyze and model large datasets with Power Pivot, an Excel add-in that provides advanced data analysis capabilities.

- Solver: Solve complex optimization problems with Solver, an Excel add-in that allows you to find the optimal solution to mathematical models and scenarios.

Conclusion

With these additional resources at your disposal, you'll be well-equipped to continue your Excel journey and expand your skills beyond the content covered in this eBook. Whether you're looking to deepen your understanding of specific topics, connect with other Excel users, or explore new tools and techniques, these resources offer valuable opportunities for growth and learning.

Master Excel 2025: Your Ultimate Guide to Mastering Functions, Formulas, and More!

Acknowledgments

We would like to express our gratitude to everyone who contributed to the creation of this eBook. Special thanks to the Publishing team at for their support and guidance throughout the writing and publishing process. We also extend our appreciation to the readers and users of this eBook for their interest and feedback.

About the Author

Passionate about empowering others to excel in Excel, I have dedicated their career to helping individuals and organizations leverage the power of spreadsheet software for data analysis, visualization, and decision-making. Through this eBook aims to share their knowledge and expertise with readers worldwide, enabling them to unlock the full potential of Excel and achieve their goals.